# CONSIDERING MARRIAGE
### Are You Fit to Be Tied?

JUNE HUNT

AspirePress

Torrance, California

Considering Marriage: Are You Fit to Be Tied?
Copyright © 2013 Hope For The Heart
All rights reserved.
Aspire Press, a division of Rose Publishing, Inc.
4733 Torrance Blvd., #259
Torrance, California 90503 USA
www.aspirepress.com

Register your book at www.aspirepress.com/register
Get inspiration via email, sign up at www.aspirepress.com

Printed in the United States of America
010513DP

# CONTENTS

𝒟ear friend,

From the beginning of time, when God said, *"It is not good for the man to be alone"* (Genesis 2:18), people have sought to find someone special with whom to share their lives. For some, marriage has been immensely meaningful, but for others, it's been pure misery.

What do you need to know before you tie the marital knot? Consider this true story about someone very dear to my heart.

This sweet-tempered, sweet-spirited college student began to date a handsome, winsome young man. He pursued. She pulled back. He pursued. She wanted time. He pursued. She left for the summer. He followed her. Shortly afterward, they were engaged and then married.

Meanwhile, I was delighted—what an attractive couple! A few years and a few children later, they divorced. *How could this be?* I wondered. Many of us were stunned, but we did not live in their home. We did not have all the facts.

*How could this be? What happened?*

While there were biblical grounds for divorce, in truth, she should never have married him in the first place. This became increasingly clear as she shared from her heart, "June, I didn't want to marry him. But he constantly pursued me, and I didn't know how to say *no.*"

And then she made this statement, justifying her decision: "I remember praying, 'God, if I'm not supposed to marry him, please stop it'—but He didn't!"

For a period of time, she lived with anger toward God, blaming Him for not answering her prayer. Yet, in effect, God had already answered. He had already revealed His will. Simply put, God had not given her peace about marrying this man. Yet she allowed herself to be "people-pressured" instead of Spirit-led.

How much better if she had possessed the strength to *"[speak] the truth in love"* (Ephesians 4:15)—the strength to say, "*No.* I think you have many wonderful traits. I like many things about you, but the type of love I have for you is not a marital love. Saying *yes* would be wrong toward you, therefore, I must say *no.*" Saying *no* when you need to say *no* requires strength of character.

If you truly desire to prepare for marriage, first yield your will to the will of God. Then, if you are considering a certain marriage partner, pray that you will be led by the peace of God. (Or pray that you will not have His supernatural peace if that person is not the right partner for you.)

Either way, be encouraged. God wants you to know His perfect will for marriage even more than you want to know it. He promises, *"If any of you lacks wisdom, [you] should ask God, who gives generously to all without finding fault, and it will be given to [you]"* (James 1:5). Therefore, I urge you to pour out your heart to the Lord regarding every aspect of your romantic relationship. Ask for His divine wisdom. When you do, remember: While God always answers our prayers, sometimes His answer is "yes," sometimes "no," and sometimes "not now."

May this book—along with earnest prayer and the wise counsel of trusted advisers— give you such godly guidance that you will know when God is leading you to say *yes* to marriage and when you need to say *no*. And on each step of your journey, may His thoughts be your thoughts as you surrender your will to His will.

Yours in the Lord's hope,

June Hunt

# CONSIDERING MARRIAGE
## Are You Fit to Be Tied?

Once upon a time an unhappy frog lived in the enchanted forest. Year after year the frog stayed in his swampy pond until the day he coaxed a beautiful princess to kiss him. In the twinkling of an eye, the ugly frog turned into a handsome prince. Then the beautiful couple married and lived happily ever after.

While children assume marriage is like a fairy tale, if you are seriously dating, you need to distinguish fact from fiction. If you believe marriage will meet all your needs or miraculously turn your marriage partner into a prince or princess, you're living in fantasyland! God's Word exhorts us to be wise about our expectations for marriage and wise about whom we let into our hearts.

> "Above all else, guard your heart,
> for it is the wellspring of life."
> (Proverbs 4:23)

# DEFINITIONS

Regret, regret, regret! How many couples choose their mates too quickly and now live their lives full of regret? In order to build a strong foundation for marriage, learn as much as possible about yourself, your future mate, and God's purpose for marriage *before* you tie the knot.

> "Do you see a man who speaks
> in haste? There is more hope
> for a fool than for him."
> (Proverbs 29:20)

Premarital counseling is practical advice given to a couple in preparation for marriage.

▶ Ministers and mentors often give spiritual, financial, and emotional guidance with special focus on relational pitfalls.

▶ Medical professionals give physical examinations and information about sexual and pregnancy issues, as well as genetic concerns.

▶ Wedding consultants primarily give guidance about the wedding ceremony and reception.

"Plans fail for lack of counsel,
but with many advisers they succeed."
(Proverbs 15:22)

QUESTION: "Instead of going through a marriage ceremony, why not elope? Undoubtedly, eloping would save a lot of money and effort."

ANSWER: A marriage ceremony, by design, is a sacred event to be performed in the midst of those who love and care about you. When you both recite the marriage vows, you make a commitment in the presence of those who will support you to keep the covenant for a lifetime! The ceremony need not be big, elaborate, or expensive.

"Come now, let's make a covenant,
you and I, and let it serve
as a witness between us."
(Genesis 31:44)

Premarital counseling involves teaching a couple open and honest communication in preparation for marriage.

▶ Communication is sharing and understanding each other, both verbally and nonverbally.

▶ Communication is listening and responding respectfully.

▶ Communication involves a willingness to be honest and vulnerable.

"The tongue that brings healing
is a tree of life, but a deceitful tongue
crushes the spirit."
(Proverbs 15:4)

**QUESTION:** "How can I be 100 percent sure that the person I marry will remain committed to me?"

**ANSWER:** You can't be 100 percent sure about the commitment of any other person, but you can commit 100 percent of yourself to the marriage and choose to stay 100 percent committed to your covenant partner. This is God's desire as revealed in His Word.

"She is your partner, the wife
of your marriage covenant. ...
So guard yourself in your spirit,
and do not break faith with the wife
[husband] of your youth."
(Malachi 2:14–15)

A couple needs to have an accurate understanding of each other's expectations and desires. *Preparation for Partnership* is an excellent exercise for opening the door to meaningful communication. Both parties should complete each sentence in writing and then talk through each point.

- My definition of love is _____
  _____

- My reason for marriage is _____
  _____

- My way of handling conflict is _____
  _____

- My way of dealing with anger is _____
  _____

- My preference for spending free time is __
  _____

- My concept of the role and
  responsibilities of a husband is _____
  _____

- My concept of the role and
  responsibilities of a wife is _____
  _____

- My views on sex within marriage are ____
  _____

- My commitments to my extended family are _____

- My commitments to my future in-laws are _____

- My expectation regarding time with friends (following marriage) is _____
_____

- My position on the use of alcohol is \_\_\_\_\_
_____

- My experience with illegal drugs is \_\_\_\_\_
_____

- My priorities for spending money are \_\_
_____

- My priorities for saving money are _____
_____

- My experience with debt and my commitment regarding debt are _____
_____

- My goals for marriage are _____

- My desires regarding children are _____
_____

- My commitment to be actively involved in a church fellowship is _____

- My spiritual goals and desires are _____
_____

"How much better to get wisdom than gold, to choose understanding rather than silver!" (Proverbs 16:16)

## WHAT IS a Christian Marriage?

A Christian marriage is a *covenant* agreement in which a man and a woman, both committed to Jesus Christ, are legally, physically, and spiritually joined as husband and wife.

▶ A covenant is a vow, a pledge, a promise.

*"When a man makes a vow to the LORD or takes an oath to obligate himself by a pledge, he must not break his word but must do everything he said."* (Numbers 30:2)

▶ A covenant is a formal, solemn binding agreement.

*"God said to Abraham, 'As for you, you must keep my covenant, you and your descendants after you for the generations to come.'"* (Genesis 17:9)

▶ A covenant that is broken displeases the Lord.

*"You flood the LORD's altar with tears. You weep and wail because he no longer pays attention to your offerings or accepts them with pleasure from your hands. You ask,*

*'Why?' It is because the* LORD *is acting as the witness between you and the wife of your youth, because you have broken faith with her, though she is your partner, the wife of your marriage covenant."* (Malachi 2:13–14)

**QUESTION: "Is there a real problem if I marry an unbeliever whom I love? I believe our love will overcome all our problems."**

**ANSWER:** Although your fiancé may have many positive qualities, you need to be realistic about the long-term ramifications of marrying a nonbeliever. Assuming you become yoked to him in marriage ...

- If he is headed toward darkness, where are you pulled?

- If he is headed toward death, where are you pulled?

- If he is headed toward destruction, where are you pulled?

The Bible says, *"Come out from them and be separate."*

**"Do not be yoked together with unbelievers. For what do righteousness and wickedness have in common? Or what fellowship can light have with darkness?**

What harmony is there between Christ and Belial? What does a believer have in common with an unbeliever? ... Therefore come out from them and be separate, says the Lord. Touch no unclean thing, and I will receive you."
(2 Corinthians 6:14–15, 17)

## WHAT ARE the Biblical Requirements for Marriage?

God designed marriage to be a committed covenant relationship between a man and a woman—a sacred, sanctified relationship of mutual love lasting for a lifetime.

▶ *Look* only to a person of the opposite sex for marriage.

*"The LORD God said: 'It is not good for the man to be alone. I will make a helper suitable for him.' ... Then the Lord God made a woman from the rib he had taken out of the man, and he brought her to the man."*
(Genesis 2:18, 22)

▶ *Leave* your lifestyle of being dependent on your parents.

*"For this reason a man will leave his father and mother ..."* (Genesis 2:24)

▶ *Link* with your mate legally.

"... *and be united to his wife* ... "
(Genesis 2:24)

▶ *Live* together as one in sexual union.

"... *and they will become one flesh.*"
(Genesis 2:24)

▶ *Love* your partner for a lifetime.

"*What God has joined together, let man not separate.*" (Mark 10:9)

**QUESTION: "I cannot financially afford to marry my fiancé. Isn't it okay for us to live together without marrying?"**

**ANSWER:** No, God set out in Scripture the right order regarding a man and a woman living together and enjoying a sexual relationship. In the second chapter of the Bible, God says a man is to leave his parents, enter into marriage, and then enjoy the sexual union. If the order is wrong, the results will be wrong.

Before you enter into marriage, you do need to have wisdom and discipline about money, both income and expenses. God not only knows your financial situation, He also knows how to meet your financial need. Your resource for wisdom and provision is your God.

> **"My God will meet all
> your needs according to his
> glorious riches in Christ Jesus."
> (Philippians 4:19)**

## WHAT IS Love?

Realistically, every marriage will have temporary dry spells in which romance and affection will wane. And, gratefully, *agape* is the love that will carry you through those times to new depths within your relationship.

> **"Love never fails."
> (1 Corinthians 13:8)**

▶ Four kinds of love (as defined in the Greek language)[1]

- *Storge*—natural affinity for another; affection

- *Eros*—emotional passion for another; romance

- *Phileo*—liking and enjoying another; friendship

- *Agape*—seeking the highest good of another; selflessness

▶What are biblical characteristics of *agape* love?

- ***Forfeit*** personal rights.

  *"This is how we know what love is: Jesus Christ laid down his life for us. And we ought to lay down our lives for our brothers."* (1 John 3:16)

- ***Focus*** on giving, not getting.

  *"For God so loved the world that he gave his one and only Son, that whoever believes in him shall not perish but have eternal life."* (John 3:16)

- ***Forgive*** personal offenses.

  *"[Love] keeps no record of wrongs."* (1 Corinthians 13:5)

**QUESTION:** "I agreed to marry someone whom I really don't want to marry. I have prayed that if God doesn't want us to marry, He will intervene. Won't God stop the marriage if it's not His will?"

**ANSWER:** No. God doesn't stop you from exercising your free will when you know a decision is against His will. In order to communicate His will to you, God either gives you peace or withholds His peace. Since God has not given you His peace, it's up to you to obey His will by not marrying this person. Don't marry anyone unless your heart has total peace.

"The peace of God,
which transcends all understanding,
will guard your hearts
and your minds in Christ Jesus."
(Philippians 4:7)

*If liking your mate is lost,
and passion is in the past,
agape is the love
that makes a marriage last!*

# CHARACTERISTIC REASONS FOR CONSIDERING MARRIAGE

From the beginning, when God said, *"It is not good for the man to be alone"* (Genesis 2:18), men and women have looked for someone with whom they can share their lives. But if a single person is searching for simply anyone to fill the void, that anyone can spell trouble!

## WHAT ARE Wrong Motives for Marriage?[2]

- "I want to marry because all my friends are getting married."

- "I want to be married because it's a couple's world."

- "I want to be married so I won't feel like a failure."

- "I want to fulfill my romantic dreams."

- "I want to get out of my painful home life."

- "I want to get even with the person who rejected me."

- "I want a better family life than I had while growing up."

- "I want to prove that I'm stable and can make a commitment."

- "I want to prove that I'm not struggling with homosexuality."

- "I want the wholesome family ideal."

- "I want to please my family."

- "I want to please my friends."

- "I want to please the person I'm dating."

- "I want to please God, who said, *'It's not good for man to be alone.'*"

- "I want to have sex whenever I desire."

- "I want to have children."

- "I want my children to grow up in a two-parent home."

- "I want someone so I won't be alone."

- "I want someone to benefit my career/ ministry."

- "I want someone to need me."

- "I want someone to make me happy."

- "I want someone to take care of me financially."

- "I want someone to take care of me emotionally."

- "I want someone with whom I can grow old."

> "All a man's ways seem right to him, but the LORD weighs the heart."
> (Proverbs 21:2)

**QUESTION:** "I'm considering marrying someone I've been dating. He has negative habits, including abusive anger, yet he seems unwilling to change. Although he is very possessive, he says I am the reason he gets angry. I love him very much, but should I continue thinking about marrying him?"

**ANSWER:** Be cautious with your heart, and be candid with your concerns. Ask if he would be willing to receive counseling for his possessiveness and excessive anger. He needs to look at the real reason for his "need" to control you, and he needs to look to God to meet his inner needs. If he is not willing—or if he receives counseling but doesn't change his behavior—he is not marriage material! To consider marriage at this time would be unwise. He is too busy blaming you for his bad behavior.

"A hot-tempered man must pay
the penalty; if you rescue him,
you will have to do it again."
(Proverbs 19:19)

**QUESTION:** "I know I've made a huge mistake—I'm pregnant, but not married! Should I get married for the sake of the baby?"

**ANSWER:** If you are considering marrying the father—or someone else—pregnancy must not be the primary reason to marry. You need to have similar commitments, goals, and values. The Bible says ...

"Do two walk together
unless they have agreed to do so?"
(Amos 3:3)

▶ Ask yourself these questions:

- Would an immediate marriage now be wise in the long term?

- Am I in a good place to consider marriage?

- Would my husband love my child and be a good role model?

- Can he financially support the baby and me?

- Does he like and want children?

- Is he someone with whom I would like to spend the rest of my life?

- Do I feel led by the Lord to marry him?

- Do we share core spiritual values?

If you are considering marriage, first obtain premarital counseling. (And be aware that 75 percent of teenage marriages end in divorce.) In order to consider marrying, you both need to have the same spiritual foundation, or your marriage may fall apart.

> **"Do not be yoked together with unbelievers. ... What fellowship can light have with darkness? ...**
> **What does a believer have in common with an unbeliever?"**
> **(2 Corinthians 6:14–15)**

**Being Guided by the Spirit of God**

The most important decision a person can make, apart from accepting Christ as Lord and Savior, is the choice of a lifelong marriage partner. And since no one but God knows the future, the wisest decision we can make is to trust our future into the hands of the Lord and literally be led by His Spirit.

> "He [the Spirit of truth]
> will guide you into all truth."
> (John 16:13)

**The Holy Spirit will guide you through ...**

▶ *Looking* at the Word of God

- **ASK:**

  "Would this marriage measure up to biblical guidelines for a Christian marriage?"

  *"The precepts of the LORD are right, giving joy to the heart. The commands of the Lord are radiant, giving light to the eyes."* (Psalm 19:8)

▶ *Leaning* on the will of God

- **ASK:**

"Would this marriage be the path the Lord desires for me to take?"

*"Trust in the LORD with all your heart and lean not on your own understanding; in all your ways acknowledge him, and he will make your paths straight."* (Proverbs 3:5–6)

▶ *Learning* from the people of God

- **ASK:**

"Would this marriage be affirmed by parents, wise friends, and church leaders?"

*"Plans fail for lack of counsel, but with many advisers they succeed."* (Proverbs 15:22)

▶ *Listening* to the Spirit of God

- **ASK:**

"Would this marriage partner be God's choice for me?"

*"The Counselor, the Holy Spirit, whom the Father will send in my name, will teach you all things."* (John 14:26)

**QUESTION:** "Recently I've been dating someone who said, 'God told me that we are to get married.' I want to please God, but I'm not attracted to him in a marital way. What should I do?"

**ANSWER:** With great sensitivity you could say, "I am honored that you would want to marry me. Since we both want to please God, we need to realize that if God intended for us to marry, He would have also told me—but He hasn't. It very well may be that God is preparing your heart for marriage. If that is His purpose, I'm confident that the Lord will bring the right person into your life, and you both will know it."

"Many are the plans in a man's heart, but it is the LORD's purpose that prevails."
(Proverbs 19:21)

# CAUSES FOR PROBLEMS IN MARRIAGE

Reality roars like a lion after the honeymoon. When marriage partners bring their unrealistic expectations into the marriage, disillusionment may begin to eat away the marital bliss. Preconceived ideas about how to relate to each other are usually formed from parental attitudes and actions. Before you begin the journey of marriage, share with each other your presumptions and expectations. This kind of communication will go a long way in helping you discern some of the adjustments required when two seek to blend their lives into one.

**"A man will leave his father and mother and be united to his wife, and they will become one flesh." (Genesis 2:24)**

- *Expecting* sexual passion to be the same as authentic love

- *Expecting* no consequences from engaging in premarital sex

- *Expecting* romance to sustain your marriage forever

- *Expecting* your mate to always need you desperately

- *Expecting* marriage to solve your personal problems

- *Expecting* to get your own way

- *Expecting* your mate to be a mind reader

- *Expecting* religious differences to be insignificant

- *Expecting* submissiveness or strong spiritual leadership from your mate

- *Expecting* to spend every holiday with your own family

- *Expecting* that children won't strain the marriage

- *Expecting* your mate to save and spend money the way you would

- *Expecting* total agreement on how the home is kept and managed

- *Expecting* communication to be natural and automatic

- *Expecting* to always be understood by your spouse

- *Expecting* to always be defended by your spouse

- *Expecting* to always be the number one priority of your spouse

- *Expecting* to change your mate's negative behavior after you are married

- *Expecting* marriage to produce maturity in your mate

- *Expecting* your in-laws to accept you individually and to approve of you as a couple

> **"You expected much, but see,
> it turned out to be little."
> (Haggai 1:9)**

**QUESTION:** "My fiancé and I are concerned that his over-controlling family will cause problems for us after we are married. How can we resolve some of these potential problems before we get married?"

**ANSWER:** You are wise to realize that any concerns about extended family problems should be addressed and resolved between the two of you *before* you marry. To help diffuse potential "in-law interference," discuss and agree on the following principles.

- Agree to the "leave and cleave" principle that establishes the two of you as united in the way you will handle in-law problems.

  *"For this reason a man will leave his father and mother and be united to his wife, and they will become one flesh."* (Genesis 2:24)

- Pursue peace whenever possible.

  *"If it is possible, as far as it depends on you, live at peace with everyone."* (Romans 12:18)

- Be humble, patient, and respectful when you are in the presence of your fiancé's family.

  *"Be completely humble and gentle; be patient, bearing with one another in love."* (Ephesians 4:2)

- Maintain a positive attitude about your fiancé's family. Don't develop a critical spirit, but look for the best in them. (Even if your fiancé is critical, you need to hold your tongue.)

*"Let your conversation be always full of grace, seasoned with salt, so that you may know how to answer everyone."* (Colossians 4:6)

In many cultures, a "red flag" means **Warning! Danger! Watch out!** The Bible offers numerous insights regarding red flag relationships, and those who are wise will heed these warnings.

> **"The wisdom of the prudent is
> to give thought to their ways,
> but the folly of fools is deception."**
> **(Proverbs 14:8)**

## Objection of Parents

### Esau

The king of the Philistines said to Isaac, Esau's father, *"We saw clearly that the LORD was with you."* But years later when Esau was forty years old, he married two Hittite women—foreign women with pagan ways who held beliefs contrary to God's ways. The Bible simply states that these wives *"were a source of grief to Isaac and Rebekah."* Parents, because of past experience, can see potential problems that their children do not have the ability to discern (Genesis chapters 25 and 26).

The Bible says, *"Listen, my son, to your father's instruction and do not forsake your mother's teaching. ... A foolish son brings grief to his*

*father and bitterness to the one who bore him"*
(Proverbs 1:8; 17:25).

## Financial Irresponsibility

### ANANIAS AND SAPPHIRA

Because of their greed and dishonesty, Ananias and Sapphira were terrible stewards of their money. Ananias kept back for himself part of the money he had pledged to give to God's work, then lied about it. Rather than exposing it, his wife substantiated the lie. They demonstrated irresponsibility with what God had given them. And as a result, God took their lives (Acts chapter 5).

The Bible says, *"Whoever can be trusted with very little can also be trusted with much, and whoever is dishonest with very little will also be dishonest with much"* (Luke 16:10).

## Excessive Anger

### SAMSON

Samson had a hair-trigger temper, combined with an impulsive, vengeful spirit. When his wife's family behaved badly toward him, he declared that he had a "right to get even." As the feuding escalated, his excessive anger drove him to kill more than a thousand of his wife's people. Although Samson was an Israelite judge, he lost not only his sight, but also his spiritual insight (Judges chapters 14 and 15).

The Bible says, *"Do not make friends with a hot-tempered man, do not associate with one easily angered"* (Proverbs 22:24).

## Wrong Priorities

### NABAL AND ABIGAIL

Nabal, whose name means "foolish," was a wealthy, self-serving man. His arrogant attitude led him to make foolish decisions. Ungrateful for David's protection, Nabal insulted David and his men, paying back their good treatment with rude and reckless snobbery. Fortunately, Nabal's insightful wife sensed the disastrous ramifications of her husband's actions. Had she not personally and graciously appealed to David, Nabal's brash words and foolish pride would have resulted in bloodshed, disaster, and utter ruin (1 Samuel chapter 25).

The Bible says, *"Stay away from a foolish man, for you will not find knowledge on his lips"* (Proverbs 14:7).

## Unequally Yoked Relationships

### SOLOMON

Once called the wisest man in the world, Solomon did something stupid. He married 700 wives—many of them foreign women. Although he knew God had forbidden him to marry outside his faith, Solomon thought he would be strong enough to withstand their heathen influence. However, in time, he compromised his devotion to the one true God and turned to his wives' pagan gods. Because Solomon chose to yoke himself to unbelievers, he lost the light of God and descended into spiritual darkness (1 Kings chapter 11).

The Bible says, *"Do not be yoked together with unbelievers. ... What fellowship can light have with darkness? ... What does a believer have in common with an unbeliever?"* (2 Corinthians 6:14–15).

## Lack of Integrity

### SAMSON AND DELILAH

Although he was one of Israel's judges, Samson was drawn into an illicit relationship with Delilah, a deceitful, Philistine woman. From the beginning, she betrayed his trust, and in return, he lied to her. Even though he knew she was not trustworthy, Samson still did not stop the relationship. Ultimately, Samson's moral weakness and lack of integrity caused his degradation, defeat and ultimate humiliation (Judges chapter 16).

The Bible says, *"The integrity of the upright guides them, but the unfaithful are destroyed by their duplicity"* (Proverbs 11:3).

## Marriage of Convenience

### DAVID AND MICHAL

King Saul considered David a serious threat to his throne. One day, after Saul discovered that his daughter Michal was in love with David, he lured the young man to perform a heroic military mission in exchange for his daughter, secretly hoping it would bring about David's death. Instead, David's mission was a great success. Now David had earned the right to marry into the royal family. However, this "marriage of convenience" for both Saul and David was merely an alliance that failed to bring harmony, for soon David's heart and eyes wandered away from home (1 Samuel 18:17–29).

The Lord says, *"Woe to the obstinate children ... to those who carry out plans that are not mine, forming an alliance, but not by my Spirit, heaping sin upon sin"* (Isaiah 30:1).

## Not Romantically Attracted

### JACOB AND LEAH

When Jacob met Rachel, he was immediately attracted to her. But in order for them to marry, he first had to marry Leah, her older sister. Leah knew she was not loved, but she hoped that, over time, Jacob would grow to love her because she bore his children. However, the romantic attraction Leah so longed for never did develop, and she never felt loved or cherished as a wife (Genesis chapters 29 and 30).

The Bible says, *"May your fountain be blessed, and may you rejoice in the wife of your youth. A loving doe, a graceful deer—may her breasts satisfy you always, may you ever be captivated by her love"* (Proverbs 5:18–19).

**QUESTION:** "Is it important to be romantically attracted to the one I intend to marry? After all, in biblical times a person's mate was chosen by a parent or by someone else."

**ANSWER:** In biblical times, fathers arranged the marriages of their children; however, today, that is typically not the case. In most situations, individuals decide for themselves whom they will marry—still desiring their parents' blessing. Whatever the cultural setting, our sovereign God is able to work His will, either by directing the hearts of the fathers or by directing the hearts of the couple. The marriage of Jacob and Leah is an example of a husband who was not attracted to his wife. He gave his body but couldn't give his heart because it had already been given to Rachel. God intends marriage to be fulfilling in every aspect (spiritually, emotionally, and physically), so it follows that He would not direct two people to marry who were not physically attracted to one another. Physical attraction is not the glue that holds a marriage together, but it definitely strengthens the glue.

**"The wife's body does not belong to her alone but also to her husband. In the same way, the husband's body does not belong to him alone but also to his wife."**
**(1 Corinthians 7:4)**

Typically, people thinking about marriage are fairly close to the same age. When two people with a wide age difference are drawn to one another, the reason is often that both are unconsciously seeking to satisfy their unmet needs from childhood. Peers who are about the same age perceive each other as equals and form relationships balanced in power. Conversely, couples with a greater disparity in age tend to perceive each other not as equals and form relationships with an imbalance of power ... that is, with one partner having more power than the other. In the following scenarios, consider what needs each person is trying to fulfill.

▶ A much *older woman* attracted to a much younger man

- What need is she trying to meet within herself?

  This woman desires to be a caregiver, a nurturer, and at times even a mother figure. In order to feel *significant*, she needs someone young whom she thinks she can control in order to feel good about herself. Sometimes, though, she picks a younger man in an attempt to recapture her youth.

▶ A much *younger man* attracted to a much older woman

- What need is he trying to meet within himself?

This man desires to be fussed over, coddled, and even mothered in order to feel *secure*. He wants to feel carefree and is allowed to stay undisciplined and irresponsible in his lifestyle.

▶ A much *older man* attracted to a much younger woman

- What need is he trying to meet within himself?

This man desires to be the ruler, the controller, and at times even the father in order to feel *significant*. He is possessive and dominating and needs a woman to display, much like a trophy, so as to feel good about himself. Sometimes, too, he picks a younger woman in an attempt to recapture his youth.

▶ A much *younger woman* attracted to a much older man

- What need is she trying to meet within herself?

This woman is looking for a provider, a protector who is more of a father figure in order to feel secure. She wants to be secure and worry free. She lives excessively dependent in order to feel *secure*. Sometimes because of an abusive background, she lives without emotional boundaries and finds it difficult for her voice to be heard.

When God created the first marriage relationship, He didn't make the woman from the man's feet so that she would be subservient to him or from his head so that she would rule over him, but from his side so that she would be equal to him.

**"Then the Lord God made a woman from the rib he had taken out of the man, and he brought her to the man."**
**(Genesis 2:22)**

A wide age difference is not always a problem, but it becomes a problem when such a difference destroys God's design for equality in marriage. A combination of *love* and *respect*, not position or power, is the cornerstone on which a godly marriage is built.

**"Each one of you also must love his wife as he loves himself, and the wife must respect her husband."**
**(Ephesians 5:33)**

**WRONG BELIEF:**

"Only in marriage will I find the love, significance, and security I need to feel complete."

**RIGHT BELIEF:**

"As a Christian, I am totally complete in Christ, whether I'm married or single. If I am to marry, God's abiding love will enable me to unselfishly love the one He has given me to marry."

**"For in Christ all the fullness of the Deity lives in bodily form, and you have been given fullness in Christ."**
**(Colossians 2:9–10)**

## Do You Want a Relationship That Lasts Forever?

Unselfish love and mutual commitment are required qualities in every intimate relationship. We all want to know we can trust the commitment and plans that are promised.

Trust is a huge issue in our relationships. You want to trust that what is promised will come true. Trust is essential in our relationship with God.

God has a plan—a promised, trustworthy plan based on His love and commitment to you. In order for you to feel secure in your relationship with the Lord, you need to know and embrace His plan for you.

## Four Points of God's Plan:

### #1 God's Purpose for You is *Salvation*.

What was God's motivation in sending Christ to earth?

To express His love for you by saving you! The Bible says ...

*"God so loved the world that he gave his one and only Son, that whoever believes in him shall not perish but have eternal life. For God did not send his Son into the world to condemn the world, but to save the world through him."* (John 3:16–17)

What was Jesus' purpose in coming to earth?

To forgive your sins, empower you to have victory over sin, and enable you to live a fulfilled life! Jesus said ...

*"I have come that they may have life, and that they may have it more abundantly."* (John 10:10 NKJV)

## #2 Your Problem is *Sin*.

What exactly is sin?

Sin is living independently of God's standard—knowing what is right, but choosing what is wrong.

*"Anyone, then, who knows the good he ought to do and doesn't do it, sins."* (James 4:17)

What is the major consequence of sin?

Spiritual death, eternal separation from God. Scripture states ...

*"Your iniquities [sins] have separated you from your God. ... For the wages of sin is death, but the gift of God is eternal life in Christ Jesus our Lord."* (Isaiah 59:2; Romans 6:23)

## #3 God's Provision for You is the *Savior*.

Can anything remove the penalty for sin?

Yes! Jesus died on the cross to personally pay the penalty for your sins. The Bible says ...

*"God demonstrates his own love for us in this: While we were still sinners, Christ died for us."* (Romans 5:8)

What is the solution to being separated from God?

Belief in (entrusting your life to) Jesus Christ as the only way to God the Father. Jesus says ...

*"I am the way and the truth and the life. No one comes to the Father except through me."* (John 14:6)

### #4 Your Part is *Surrender*.

Give Christ control of your life, entrusting yourself to Him.

*"Jesus said to his disciples, 'If anyone would come after me, he must deny himself and take up his cross [die to your own self-rule] and follow me. For whoever wants to save his life will lose it, but whoever loses his life for me will find it. What good will it be for a man if he gains the whole world, yet forfeits his soul?'"* (Matthew 16:24–26)

Place your faith in (rely on) Jesus Christ as your personal Lord and Savior and reject your "good works" as a means of earning God's approval.

*"It is by grace you have been saved, through faith—and this not from yourselves, it is the gift of God—not by works, so that no one can boast."* (Ephesians 2:8–9)

The moment you choose to receive Jesus as your Lord and Savior—entrusting your life to Him—He comes to live inside you. Then He gives you His power to live the fulfilled life God has planned for you. If you want to be fully forgiven by God and become the person God created you to be, you can tell Him in a simple, heartfelt prayer like this:

### PRAYER OF SALVATION

*"God, I want a real relationship with You—an eternal union.*
*I admit that many times I've chosen to go my own way instead of Your way.*
*Please forgive me for my sins.*
*Jesus, thank You for dying on the cross to pay the penalty for my sins.*
*Come into my life to be my Lord and my Savior.*
*Change me from the inside out and make me the person You created me to be.*
*In Your holy name I pray.*
*Amen."*

## What Can You Expect Now?

If you sincerely prayed this prayer, look at what God says about your relationship with Him.

"The Lᴏʀᴅ himself goes before you and will be with you; he will never leave you nor forsake you. Do not be afraid; do not be discouraged."
(Deuteronomy 31:8)

# STEPS TO SOLUTION

Couples who desire to please the Lord have already been given a picture of God's design for the marital relationship. The Bible tells us that marriage is to reflect the sacrificial love that Christ has for His bride, the church. Although the backgrounds of a husband and wife may be different and their expectations may conflict, they can develop unity of heart through mutual submission and godly respect.

> "Submit one to another
> out of reverence for Christ. ...
> Each one of you [husbands]
> also must love his wife as he loves
> himself, and the wife must
> respect her husband."
> (Ephesians 5:21, 33)

## KEY VERSE TO MEMORIZE

*"And this is my prayer:
that your love may abound
more and more in knowledge and depth
of insight, so that you may be able to
discern what is best
and may be pure and blameless
until the day of Christ."*
(Philippians 1:9–10)

## KEY PASSAGE TO READ

*"Love is patient, love is kind.
It does not envy, it does not boast,
it is not proud. It is not rude, it is not
self-seeking, it is not easily angered, it
keeps no record of wrongs. Love does
not delight in evil but rejoices with the
truth. It always protects, always trusts,
always hopes, always perseveres."*
(1 Corinthians 13:4–7)

You will learn much about the maturity of your fiancé, about your relationship, and about yourself if you both take **The True Love Test** based on 1 Corinthians chapter 13. This will help you evaluate your readiness for intimacy in marriage.

Each of you should fill out both lists and then discuss your answers, circling "Y" for *Yes* and "N" for *No*.

---

| | | |
|---|---|---|
| Y | N | I am patient with you and with others. |
| Y | N | I am kind to you and to others. |
| Y | N | I am envious of you or of others. |
| Y | N | I am boastful around you or around others. |
| Y | N | I am prideful around you or around others. |
| Y | N | I am rude to you or to others. |
| Y | N | I am self-seeking. |
| Y | N | I am easily angered. |

| | | |
|---|---|---|
| Y | N | I am keeping a record of wrongs. |
| Y | N | I am delighted when you or others fail. |
| Y | N | I am truthful with you and with others. |
| Y | N | I am protective of you. |
| Y | N | I am trusting of you. |
| Y | N | I am full of hope for you. |
| Y | N | I am faithful to persevere through problems with you and with others. |

---

| | | |
|---|---|---|
| Y | N | You are patient with others and with me. |
| Y | N | You are kind to others and to me. |
| Y | N | You are envious of others or of me. |
| Y | N | You are boastful around others or around me. |
| Y | N | You are prideful around others or around me. |

| | | |
|---|---|---|
| Y | N | You are rude to others or to me. |
| Y | N | You are self-seeking. |
| Y | N | You are easily angered. |
| Y | N | You are keeping a record of wrongs. |
| Y | N | You are delighted when I or others fail. |
| Y | N | You are truthful with others and with me. |
| Y | N | You are protective of me. |
| Y | N | You are trusting of me. |
| Y | N | You are full of hope for me. |
| Y | N | You are faithful to persevere through problems with me and with others. |

**QUESTION:** "My fiancé has difficulty talking about his feelings. How can I help him open up and share his hopes, dreams, and expectations for marriage?"

**ANSWER:** If communication is not established before marriage, you may both wake up afterward and discover you don't have much in common. Therefore, seek advice from an older, mature couple. Find a church that offers premarital counseling. Make a list of topics for both of you to address. Ask married couples which issues they wish they had discussed prior to marriage.

"The heart of the discerning
acquires knowledge;
the ears of the wise seek it out."
(Proverbs 18:15)

The book of Ruth lays out godly character traits for men and women who are "marriage material."

For example:

## Admirable Men (Like Boaz)

▶Financially responsible .................... Ruth 2:1

▶Strong in leadership ................................. 2:5

▶Protective ................................................. 2:9

▶Focused in character ................................2:11

▶Generous ................................................. 2:12

▶Compassionate ........................................2:15

▶Decisive ...................................................3:11

▶Trustworthy ............................................3:14

▶Industrious ........................................... 4:1–4

▶Committed .......................................... 4:9–10

## Admirable Women (Like Ruth)

▶ Diligent ............................................Ruth 2:2

▶ Submissive .......................................2:22–23

▶ Wise..................................................3:10

▶ Virtuous............................................3:11

▶ Unselfish ..........................................2:18

▶ Grateful.............................................2:10

▶ Courageous ...................................... 3:1–3, 5

▶ Trusting ............................................ 3:7–8

▶ Hardworking.................................... 2:6

▶ Committed ........................................1:16

## The "Great Mate" Checklist

Since no one is perfect, selecting a "perfect marriage partner" is impossible. But certain questions can help you determine whether or not a person would be a great mate. For example, an excellent predictor of the future is wrapped up in the question, How does he treat his mother? or How does she treat her father? The following checklist is composed of other questions that will help in the selection of a great mate. (Indicate *yes* with a (✓) checkmark.)

☐ Is this someone for whom I feel total peace about marrying?

☐ Is this someone who is growing spiritually?

☐ Is this someone whose values I greatly respect?

☐ Is this someone with whom I can communicate honestly?

☐ Is this someone who handles hurt and disappointments constructively, refusing to become bitter?

☐ Is this someone who stewards time, talents, and resources responsibly?

- [ ] Is this someone who desires sexual purity?
- [ ] Is this someone who has a joyful heart, and not a critical spirit?
- [ ] Is this someone capable of a lifelong commitment?
- [ ] Is this someone who loves God first and then loves me?
- [ ] Is this someone who does not depend solely on me for happiness?
- [ ] Is this someone who values the life God has given each of us?
- [ ] Is this someone who is honest and law-abiding?
- [ ] Is this someone who has a heart to do what is best for me?
- [ ] Is this someone who demonstrates wisdom and discernment in decisions, both large and small?
- [ ] Is this someone who honors and shows respect to both of our parents?
- [ ] Is this someone who is flexible and willing to make adjustments?
- [ ] Is this someone who "fights fairly"?

- ☐ Is this someone with whom I can laugh and cry?

- ☐ Is this someone who reads God's Word and prays with me now?

- ☐ Is this someone with whom I strongly desire to share the rest of my life?

**"If you have any encouragement from being united with Christ, if any comfort from his love, if any fellowship with the Spirit, if any tenderness and compassion, then make my joy complete by being like-minded, having the same love, being one in spirit and purpose." (Philippians 2:1–2)**

**QUESTION:** "Is it ever right to break an engagement after the invitations have gone out, all the wedding plans have been made and many gifts have already been received? What can I say?"

**ANSWER:** It is never too late to do what is right. No matter what has been said or done, don't do what is wrong. You are not married until you are married, so everything that precedes the marriage commitment is neither binding nor obligatory. If you are walking down the aisle, yet know in your heart that what you are about to do is wrong, stop!

Whether others understand or not, if it's wrong for you, it's wrong for everyone involved, including your fiancé. Simply say, "God has not given me a peace about this marriage. I pray you will be able to forgive me for going this far with the wedding plans. I kept thinking my heart would change, but it hasn't. I know you cannot see it now, but if stopping is right for me, it is also right for you. If we married now, we would both come to regret it, and I know that is not what either of us wants. Doing what is right will, in the long run, give us both peace."

*"The fruit of righteousness [doing what is right] will be peace; the effect of righteousness will be quietness and confidence forever."* (Isaiah 32:17)

▶ *Don't* live in your past.

*Do* look for the positive in the present.

*"Forget the former things; do not dwell on the past. See, I am doing a new thing!"* (Isaiah 43:18–19)

▶ *Don't* focus on your fiancé's past mistakes.

*Do* focus on the evidence of a changed life, including the fruit of the Spirit. (See Galatians 5:22–23.)

*"Hatred stirs up dissension, but love covers over all wrongs."* (Proverbs 10:12)

▶ *Don't* try to change your fiancé.

*Do* look for evidence that your fiancé has a teachable attitude and a heart willing to be conformed to the character of Christ.

*"Accept one another, then, just as Christ accepted you, in order to bring praise to God."* (Romans 15:7)

▶ *Don't* expect your fiancé to meet all your needs.

*Do* expect God to be your primary Need-Meeter.

*"My God will meet all your needs according to his glorious riches in Christ Jesus."* (Philippians 4:19)

▶ ***Don't*** expect oneness to be equivalent to sameness.

***Do*** aim for unity while accepting that no two people always think the same.

*"May the God who gives endurance and encouragement give you a spirit of unity among yourselves as you follow Christ Jesus, so that with one heart and mouth you may glorify the God and Father of our Lord Jesus Christ."* (Romans 15:5–6)

▶ ***Don't*** criticize your fiancé's parents.

***Do*** speak about them with kindness and understanding.

*"Do not let any unwholesome talk come out of your mouths, but only what is helpful for building others up according to their needs, that it may benefit those who listen."* (Ephesians 4:29)

▶ ***Don't*** nag your fiancé.

***Do*** make your position clear, commit it to prayer, then watch for needed behavior change.

*"A quarrelsome wife is like a constant dripping."* (Proverbs 19:13)

▶ **Don't** joke about sexual promiscuity.

**Do** see sexual intimacy as a picture of the holy union between Christ and His bride, the church.

*"Among you there must not be even a hint of sexual immorality, or of any kind of impurity, or of greed, because these are improper for God's holy people. Nor should there be obscenity, foolish talk or coarse joking, which are out of place, but rather thanksgiving."* (Ephesians 5:3–4)

▶ **Don't** joke about divorce as an option.

**Do** eliminate the word *divorce* from your vocabulary. God hates divorce!

*"'I hate divorce,' says the Lord God. ... So guard yourself in your spirit, and do not break faith."* (Malachi 2:16)

▶ **Don't** rationalize, "It's okay to have sex— we're engaged, and we'll be married soon."

**Do** realize that sexual responsibility before marriage demonstrates that you will be sexually responsible after marriage. And statistically, sexual impurity prior to marriage increases the odds of divorce after marriage.

*"For God did not call us to be impure, but to live a holy life."* (1 Thessalonians 4:7)

▶ ***Don't*** disregard a check in your spirit.

***Do*** talk with someone who knows you and your fiancé well in order to discern the cause of your uneasiness, then wait for God's confirmation. Do not marry without the peace of God.

*"I will instruct you and teach you in the way you should go; I will counsel you and watch over you."* (Psalm 32:8)

Preparing for a wedding requires careful planning and preparation. But amidst all of the excitement, it is easy for couples to get caught up in perfecting the details of their big day while failing to lay an adequate foundation for a marriage relationship designed to last a lifetime.

If you are aiming for a marriage relationship that honors God, is mutually satisfying, and will stand the test of time—take these steps to reach the target.

### Reaching the Target

▶ **Target #1.** *A New Purpose:* God's purpose for me is to be conformed to the character of Christ.

*"Those God foreknew he also predestined to be conformed to the likeness of his Son."* (Romans 8:29)

"I'll do whatever it takes to be conformed to the character of Christ."

▶ **Target #2.** *A New Priority:* God's priority for me is to change my thinking.

*"Do not conform any longer to the pattern of this world, but be transformed by the renewing of your mind."* (Romans 12:2)

"I'll do whatever it takes to line up my thinking with God's thinking.

▶**Target #3.** *A New Plan:* God's plan for me is to rely on Christ's strength, not my strength, to be all He created me to be.

*"I can do all things through Christ who strengthens me."* (Philippians 4:13 NKJV)

"I'll do whatever it takes to fulfill His plan in His strength."

## My Personalized Plan

### 1 Admit My Need

I admit that while I may think I can do a great job of selecting my future mate—based solely on my own insight and understanding—I'm unable to do so. Only God knows each of us perfectly. He alone knows what lies ahead for me and the one I love. The only way I can make a right decision is to be guided by Him.

*"Trust in the LORD with all your heart and lean not on your own understanding; in all your ways acknowledge him, and he will make your paths straight."* (Proverbs 3:5–6)

## 2 Ground Myself in Reality

I refuse to ignore red flags and "checks" in my spirit related to my decision to marry. If I have concerns, I will pursue them until I have answers, clarity, and peace. I refuse to embrace "magical thinking" in the hopes that if I ignore what concerns me, it will simply go away. I will acknowledge what concerns, frustrates, and irritates me about the one I'm considering for marriage, knowing that these things will be greatly amplified if we marry.

*"The prudent see danger and take refuge, but the simple keep going and suffer for it."* (Proverbs 27:12)

## 3 Get Healthy

I will hold myself accountable for addressing my own emotional wounds, unpacking my emotional baggage, and becoming as emotionally and spiritually whole as possible before I marry, and I will hold the one I care for accountable for doing the same. This may include forgiving those who have hurt either of us in the past, grieving significant losses, attending recovery classes that address unresolved issues from childhood, and any other inner work necessary to be as healthy as possible.

*"Physical training is of some value, but godliness has value for all things, holding promise for both the present life and the life to come."* (1 Timothy 4:8)

## 4 Acknowledge the Importance of Stewardship

Being aware that money is one of the most common reasons for divorce, I will thoroughly investigate my fiancé's financial position, practices, and attitudes. I will not rationalize that doing so is unwarranted or unromantic or that our love will overcome any financial concerns or failings. If either one of us is in debt, we will resolve either to be debt free or to have a written, realistic plan to be debt free before we marry.

*"Let no debt remain outstanding, except the continuing debt to love one another."* (Romans 13:8)

## 5 Take Time

I will give myself time to get to know my fiancée and won't allow people or circumstances to shortcut this vital process. If we don't live in the same city, I will make every effort to rectify that so that we can benefit from seeing each other regularly and in a wide assortment of circumstances, not just on weekends when we are both on our best behavior.

If I am divorced: Before remarriage I will give myself sufficient time to grieve, to examine my role in the failed marriage, and to heal. (Note: Everyone heals and recovers from a broken marriage at their own pace. A longer marriage will likely require a longer recovery. Counseling literature suggests a range of recommended "waiting periods" before remarriage from one month of singleness for every year of marriage to one year of singleness for every five years of marriage.)

*"Those who hope in the LORD will renew their strength. They will soar on wings like eagles; they will run and not grow weary, they will walk and not be faint."* (Isaiah 40:31)

## 6 Be Biblical

If either of us is divorced, I will seek the Lord and godly counsel to determine whether we have scriptural grounds for remarriage.

*"In his heart a man plans his course, but the Lord determines his steps."* (Proverbs 16:9)

## 7 Disagree Well

I resolve to not marry a person with whom I have not had ample experience working through conflict productively. I will recognize that not having differences of opinion and disagreements before marriage is not a healthy sign, rather it is a signal that we do not know each other well enough yet to be ourselves and speak our minds. Rather than sidestepping necessary confrontation and conflict during dating, I will welcome it as an opportunity to learn to "fight fair."

*"Speaking the truth in love, we will in all things grow up into him who is the Head, that is, Christ."* (Ephesians 4:15)

## Sexual Purity for Courtship and Engagement

Successful marriages are built on a foundation of trust. Trust flourishes when couples demonstrate they have one another's highest and best interest at heart, for this is the essence of true love. Premarital sex is not God's will and is not in the best interest of unmarried couples. Therefore, true love waits.

**To maintain purity during your courtship or engagement:**

▶ Make a commitment to God and each other to maintain sexual purity until marriage. Pray about this daily and before each date. Should you ever violate this commitment, have an understanding you will break off the engagement and seek individual counsel and healing.

▶ Have same-sex "his and her" accountability partners who ask explicit questions about sexual purity on a weekly basis—or more often if needed. Give them a copy of your written sexual purity commitment. (See page 74).

▶ Let your accountability partners know when you will be alone together in private for an extended period. Ask them to lift you up in prayer at these times.

**"Marriage should be honored by all, and the marriage bed kept pure, for God will judge the adulterer and all the sexually immoral."**
**(Hebrews 13:4)**

## Our Purity Covenant

In obedience to God's perfect Word …

*"As obedient children, do not conform to the evil desires you had when you lived in ignorance. But just as he who called you is holy, so be holy in all you do; for it is written: 'Be holy, because I am holy.'"* (1 Peter 1:14–16)

*"For this very reason, make every effort to add to your faith goodness; and to goodness, knowledge; and to knowledge, self-control; and to self-control, perseverance; and to perseverance, godliness; and to godliness, brotherly kindness; and to brotherly kindness, love. For if you possess these qualities in increasing measure, they will keep you from being ineffective and unproductive in your knowledge of our Lord Jesus Christ."* (2 Peter 1:5–8)

*"Finally, brothers, whatever is true, whatever is noble, whatever is right, whatever is pure, whatever is lovely, whatever is admirable—if anything is excellent or praiseworthy—think about such things."* (Philippians 4:8)

*"It is God's will that you should be sanctified: that you should avoid sexual immorality; that each of you should learn to control his own body in a way that is holy and honorable, not in passionate lust like the heathen, who do not know God; and that in this matter no one should*

*wrong his brother or take advantage of him. The Lord will punish men for all such sins, as we have already told you and warned you. For God did not call us to be impure, but to live a holy life. Therefore, he who rejects this instruction does not reject man but God, who gives you his Holy Spirit."* (1 Thessalonians 4:3–8)

I promise to protect your sexual purity from this day forward. Because I respect you and honor you, I commit to building up the inner person of your heart rather than violating you.

> **"So I strive always to keep my conscience clear before God and man." (Acts 24:16)**

I pledge to show my love for you in ways that allow both of us to maintain a clear conscience before God and each other. This is my promise of purity.

Signed _____

Signed _____

Witness _____

Witness _____

Dated _____

**QUESTION:** "What do you do if both you and the one you love are Christians, yet your non-Christian parents disapprove of the person you have chosen to marry?"

**ANSWER:** God can speak through the counsel of non-Christian authorities—even in adulthood. Consider this approach:

- Ask for their candid concerns.

- Instead of being defensive, repeat back what was said, "Are you saying ... ?"

- Then ask, "What suggestions do you have ... (for him, for me, for our situation)?"

The best way to demonstrate your Christian commitment to non-believing parents is to respectfully present your appeal, but ultimately be willing to take their counsel seriously. Most parents know their children intimately, and they can sense why the marriage could be destructive.

> "Listen, my son, to your father's instruction and do not forsake your mother's teaching."
> (Proverbs 1:8)

Commit to the following plan to maximize your spiritual growth as a couple.

▶ *We commit* our lives to Jesus Christ and submit to His control.

*"If anyone would come after me, he must deny himself and take up his cross daily and follow me."* (Luke 9:23)

▶ *We commit* our home to God and pledge to make it Christ-centered.

*"Choose for yourselves this day whom you will serve. ... But as for me and my household, we will serve the LORD."* (Joshua 24:15)

▶ *We commit* our bodies to each other, and vow to be sexually faithful.

*"Marriage should be honored by all, and the marriage bed kept pure, for God will judge the adulterer and all the sexually immoral."* (Hebrews 13:4)

▶ *We commit* our finances to God, and will honor Him with our tithe.

*"'Bring the whole tithe into the storehouse, that there may be food in my house. Test me in this,' says the LORD Almighty, 'and see if I will not throw open the floodgates of heaven*

*and pour out so much blessing that you will not have room enough for it."* (Malachi 3:10)

▶ *We **commit*** to reading the Bible and praying with each other daily.

*"Your word is a lamp to my feet and a light for my path. I have taken an oath and confirmed it, that I will follow your righteous laws."* (Psalm 119:105–106)

▶ *We **commit*** to not going to bed until we have resolved—or committed to resolve— our anger.

*"'In your anger do not sin:' Do not let the sun go down while you are still angry."* (Ephesians 4:26)

▶ *We **commit*** to nurturing each other through loving encouragement.

*"And let us consider how we may spur one another on toward love and good deeds."* (Hebrews 10:24)

▶ *We **commit*** to admitting our weaknesses and to seeking prayer support, godly counsel, and accountability in order to change.

*"Therefore confess your sins to each other and pray for each other so that you may be healed. The prayer of a righteous man is powerful and effective."* (James 5:16)

▶ *We commit* to growing with each other into a deeper relationship with the Lord.

*"Let us draw near to God with a sincere heart in full assurance of faith, having our hearts sprinkled to cleanse us from a guilty conscience and having our bodies washed with pure water. Let us hold unswervingly to the hope we profess, for he who promised is faithful."* (Hebrews 10:22–23)

Signed _____

Signed _____

Witness _____

Dated _____

The following contract will help you and your fiancé process and learn from your negative emotions.

▶ **We agree** to set a time to talk when either becomes upset.

*"The purposes of a man's heart are deep waters, but a man of understanding draws them out."* (Proverbs 20:5)

▶ **We agree** to pray individually before we come together to talk.

*"Is any one of you in trouble? He should pray. Is anyone happy? Let him sing songs of praise. ... Therefore confess your sins to each other and pray for each other so that you may be healed. The prayer of a righteous man is powerful and effective."* (James 5:13, 16)

▶ **We agree** not to act out our angry feelings.

*"A fool gives full vent to his anger, but a wise man keeps himself under control."* (Proverbs 29:11)

▶ **We agree** to seek to understand the reasons for each other's thoughts and actions.

*"He who gets wisdom loves his own soul; he who cherishes understanding prospers."* (Proverbs 19:8)

▶ *We agree* to accept suggestions for changing the way we respond.

*"A prudent man sees danger and takes refuge, but the simple keep going and suffer for it."* (Proverbs 22:3)

▶ *We agree* to forgive one another completely.

- We will choose not to dwell on the offense or mentally replay it.

- We will choose not to bring it up again (manipulation).

- We will choose not to repeat it to others (slander).

*"Be kind and compassionate to one another, forgiving each other, just as in Christ God forgave you."* (Ephesians 4:32)

▶ *We agree* to seek a wise, godly mediator who is objective if we cannot come to an agreement.

*"Plans fail for lack of counsel, but with many advisers they succeed."* (Proverbs 15:22)

Signed _____

Signed _____

Witness _____

Dated _____

When we reach an impasse during conflict, we agree to the following actions.

▶ *We agree* to go first to God with our problem.

- Seek discernment from God and come to a mutual agreement on the true problem.

- Seek guidance from God's Word, asking, "Has God spoken about this anywhere in His Word?"

- Seek God's will through prayer.

*"Do not be anxious about anything, but in everything, by prayer and petition, with thanksgiving, present your requests to God. And the peace of God, which transcends all understanding, will guard your hearts and your minds in Christ Jesus."* (Philippians 4:6–7)

▶ *We agree* to negotiate a solution.

- Make a joint list of all our options.

- Individually mark each option as ...

  (P) Possible          (I) Impossible

- Evaluate all the *P*s and jointly choose the best option.

▶ **We agree**, if all options cancel out, to ...

- Delay making a decision until there is unity or until a decision must be made.

  *"I waited patiently for the LORD; he turned to me and heard my cry."* (Psalm 40:1)

- Seek the godly counsel of others.

  *"Plans fail for lack of counsel, but with many advisers they succeed."* (Proverbs 15:22)

- Trust in the sovereignty of God.

  *"We know that in all things God works for the good of those who love him, who have been called according to his purpose."* (Romans 8:28)

Signed _____

Signed _____

Witness _____

Dated _____

As you prepare for marriage, it is important for your primary goal in communication to be: "How can I meet the love needs of my fiancé?" Do you know what specific language fills the emotional needs of your beloved? Are you aware of the meaningful expressions of affection that fill up your own cup?

Selfless behavior and self-disclosure are like sugar and cream, the flavor enhancements to deeper and more intimate communication. You and your fiancé need one or more of these expressions of sincere love in order for life to "taste good"!

▶ *Time:* A healthy dose of opportunities for intimate interaction (both quantity and quality of time)

- Undivided, focused attention: Put the newspaper down.

- Eye contact: "I love you" seen from across the room.

- Listening without giving advice: No formulas for fixing it, please.

- Togetherness activities: "Let's go for a walk."

- Physical presence: "I like having you around."

**Biblical Example:**

Mary sitting at the feet of Jesus
(Read Luke 10:38–42.)

*"Jesus ... came to a village where a woman named Martha opened her home to him. She had a sister called Mary, who sat at the Lord's feet listening to what he said."* (Luke 10:38–39)

▶ *Talk:* Compliments and words that affirm or build up

- Words of affirmation: "Our relationship is important to me."

- Verbal compliments: "You did a great job on this meal."

- Encouragement: "I've noticed that you write thoughtful notes and letters."

- Words of appreciation: "I really appreciate your cleaning up the garage."

- Words spoken kindly: "I love you. Will you please forgive me?"

**Biblical Example:**

Parable of a tree and its fruit
(Read Luke 6:43–45.)

*"Out of the overflow of his heart his mouth speaks."* (Luke 6:45)

▶ **Tasks**: Doing things that are meaningful to one another

- Acts of serving one another: Pitching in when help is needed.

- Doing chores together: Cooking, cleaning, yard work, or running errands.

- Recognizing when there is a need: "You're feeling bad. Let me clean up."

- Discerning the "right" things to do: What is most meaningful to the other person, rather than to you?

- Serving your loved one's extended family: "I'll sit with your grandmother in the hospital."

**Biblical Example:**

The good Samaritan
(Read Luke 10:30–37.)

*"A man ... fell into the hands of robbers. They stripped him of his clothes, beat him and went away, leaving him half dead. ... A Samaritan, as he traveled, came where the man was; and when he saw him, he took pity on him. He went to him and bandaged his wounds, pouring on oil and wine. Then he*

*... took him to an inn and took care of him."*
(Luke 10:30, 33–34)

▶ *Tokens*: Giving gifts as visual symbols of love

- Communicate love and affection through giving gifts.

- Discern what kind of gifts are most desired, not what you would desire.

- Gifts should never be used as a bribe or have strings attached.

- Cost is not the issue unless it is way out of line with the available resources.

- Tokens of love can also be written notes of admiration and encouragement.

### Biblical Example:

The widow's mite
(Read Luke 21:1–4.)

*" ... she [the poor widow] out of her poverty put in all she had to live on."* (Luke 21:4)

▶ *Touch*: Tender and loving, physical contact

- Kissing and embracing often

- Appropriate hugs

- Holding hands

- Back and foot rubs

- A hand on the shoulder or a pat on the back

**Biblical Example:**

Jesus anointed by a sinful woman.
(Read Luke 7:36–38.)

*"A woman who had lived a sinful life ... brought an alabaster jar of perfume, and as she stood behind him [Jesus] at his feet weeping, she began to wet his feet with her tears. Then she wiped them with her hair, kissed them and poured perfume on them."*
(Luke 7:37–38)

**QUESTION: "How do I discover my fiancé's language of love?"[5]**

**ANSWER:** Ask yourself ...

- "What complaints do I hear the most in regard to what I am not doing?"

- "What am I often requested to do?"

- "How does my loved one show love to others?"

- "Have I lovingly asked what is most meaningful?"

**"A word aptly spoken is like apples
of gold in settings of silver."
(Proverbs 25:11)**

**The best marriage bond is this:**

*Two people, each personally
committed to Jesus Christ,
and together committed to each other.*

—June Hunt

# SCRIPTURES TO MEMORIZE

Am I choosing a **believer** as my lifelong mate?

> *"Do not be yoked together with unbelievers. For what do righteousness and wickedness have in common? Or what fellowship can light have with darkness? ... What does a **believer** have in common with an unbeliever?"* (2 Corinthians 6:14–15)

Are we committed to **sexual purity** and fidelity for a lifetime?

> *"Marriage should be honored by all, and the marriage bed kept **pure**, for God will judge the adulterer and all the **sexually** immoral."* (Hebrews 13:4)

Does either of us have a **fear** of the other's anger?

> *"There is no **fear** in love. But perfect love drives out fear, because fear has to do with punishment. The one who fears is not made perfect in love."* (1 John 4:18)

Are we both willing to **submit to each other's** desire?

*"**Submit to one another** out of reverence for Christ."* (Ephesians 5:21)

Do we both give **honor to our parents**?

*"'**Honor your father and your mother**, so that you may live long in the land the LORD your God is giving you.'"* (Exodus 20:12)

Are we both emotionally ready to **leave our parents**?

*"A man will **leave his father and mother** and be united to his wife, and they will become one flesh."* (Genesis 2:24)

Have we both displayed **integrity** in little and big situations?

*"The **integrity** of the upright guides them, but the unfaithful are destroyed by their duplicity."* (Proverbs 11:3)

Can we be **rebuked** by each other without becoming angry?

*"Better is open **rebuke** than hidden love. Wounds from a friend can be trusted, but an enemy multiplies kisses."* (Proverbs 27:5–6)

Are we both careful to make **wise** choices?

*"Be very careful, then, how you live–not as unwise but as **wise**."* (Ephesians 5:15)

Are we both independently **walking in God's truth**?

*"Teach me your way, O Lord, and I will **walk in your truth**; give me an undivided heart, that I may fear your name."* (Psalm 86:11)

# NOTES

1. For this section see H. Norman Wright, *So You're Getting Married* (Ventura, CA: Regal, 1985), 56–63.

2. For this section see Bill Hybels and Lynne Hybels, *Fit to Be Tied* (Grand Rapids: Zondervan, 1991), 30–31; Wright, *So You're Getting Married*, 7.

3. Wright, *So You're Getting Married*, 248.

4. Gary Chapman identifies the five love languages as Words of Affirmation, Quality Time, Receiving Gifts, Acts of Service, and Physical Touch see Gary Chapman, *The Five Love Languages: The Secret to Love that Lasts* (Chicago: Northfield, 2010), 173–174.

5. Chapman, *The Five Love Languages*, 173–175.

## SELECTED BIBLIOGRAPHY

Elliot, Elisabeth. *Passion and Purity: Learning to Bring Your Love Life Under Christ's Control*. Grand Rapids: Fleming H. Revell, 1984.

Fryling, Alice, and Robert Fryling. *A Handbook for Engaged Couples: A Communication Tool for Those About to Be Married*. 2nd ed. Downers Grove, IL: InterVarsity, 1996.

Hunt, June. *Seeing Yourself Through God's Eyes*. Eugene, OR: Harvest House Publishers, 2008.

Hybels, Bill, and Lynne Hybels. *Fit to Be Tied*. Grand Rapids: Zondervan, 1991.

Mace, David R. *Getting Ready for Marriage*. Rev. ed. Nashville: Abingdon, 1985.

Mack, Wayne A., and Nathan A. Mack. *Preparing for Marriage God's Way*. Tulsa, OK: Virgil Hensley, 1986.

McGinnis, Alan Loy. *The Romance Factor*. New York: HarperSanFrancisco, 1990.

Wright, H. Norman. *So You're Getting Married*. Ventura, CA: Regal, 1985.

Wright, H. Norman, and Wes Roberts. *Before You Say "I Do": A Marriage Preparation Manual for Couples*. Rev. and expanded ed. Eugene, OR: Harvest House, 1997.

June Hunt's HOPE FOR THE HEART booklets are biblically-based, and full of practical advice that is relevant, spiritually-fulfilling and wholesome. Each topic presents scriptural truths and examples of real-life situations to help readers relate and integrate June's counseling guidance into their own lives. Practical for individuals from all walks of life, this new booklet series invites readers into invaluable restoration, emotional health, and spiritual freedom.

## HOPE FOR THE HEART TITLES

**www.aspirepress.com**

## The HOPE FOR THE HEART Biblical Counseling Library is Your Solution!

- Easy-to-read, perfect for anyone.
- Short. Only 92 pages. Good for the busy person.
- Christ-centered biblical advice and practical help
- Tested and proven over 20 years of June Hunt's radio ministry
- 25 titles in the series – each tackling a key issue people face today.
- Affordable. You or your church can give away, lend, or sell them.

Display available for churches and ministries.

**www.aspirepress.com**